Sale of this book without a front cover may be unauthorized. If this book is coverless, it may have been reported to the publisher as "unsold or destroyed" and neither the author nor the publisher may have received payment for it.

Copyright © Helen Stone. All rights reserved.
Photographs © Debbie Lane. All rights reserved
ISBN 978-1-4710-5046-6

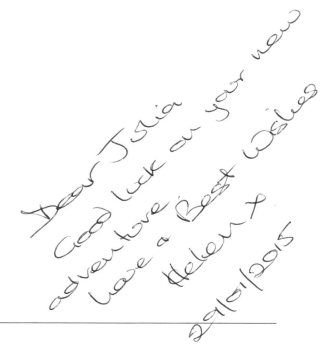

EMOTIONAL TIDES

Body Language

This body language that we both evolve
Is something that I cannot resolve
It touches somewhere deep inside
Where neither you nor I can hide

For what do I want to hear or say
Is a fear of losing or going away
I have never felt this longing before
In love and life there is always war

I sometimes wonder where we're going
Life's pleasures enable us for growing
For if we are to become anymore
We have to gain from experiences that we saw

Our destinies cross but are they to join
Heads or Tails as we flip the coin
Whatever the outcome we can change
Just open the book and turn the page

No matter that we have each other
How strong is our need for one another
We can use our mind, body and souls
To achieve one another's ultimate goals

Life's Ups and Down

I sometimes wonder what it's all about
The way life deals its ups and downs
Always viewing it through rose tinted glasses
Yet feeling the emotion as it passes

I look at myself in a deeper way
Understanding now what I have to say
I have stepped off that fantasy plane
To get my life back together again

Looking straight into the face of reality
I actually feel immense tranquility
Finally reaching a needed balance
This I owe to you with heartfelt thanks

Friends are what we need most
People who care and love unconditionally
When I'm with you there's no need to boast
To be myself around you means the utmost

I have therefore nothing left to say
Except a deep respect for you understanding me
Remember friendship is a two way thing
So don't hesitate to give me a ring

Friendship

Friendship I heard myself say
That's what I said I don't know why
Never wanting to scare you away
I find myself looking up at the sky
Thinking shall I continue as I do
Or say what I feel and maybe look a fool

Commitment you don't need, right now neither do I
To me, I don't want you to say goodbye
I know I am taking a risk when I speak
I can't leave it any longer, the truth I seek
So I am saying now what I should have said that night
A link between us that just feels so right

Your eyes and soul are touching me so deep
You are there for me when my eyes do weep
When you lie beside me I feel warm inside
My emotions I no longer refuse to hide
In you I have found what I have been looking for
So now you finally know the score

I understand if you have to push me away
I don't want you to feel you have to stay
Be honest with me that is all I ask
Realising I know it is no easy task
My heart and mind just need to know
Which way we will eventually go

So when the talking is finally done
And I am aware of what you are feeling
I know that the past has now gone
Whatever you say the future is for living
If nothing else I have found a soul mate
My life I leave unto the hands of fate

Speaking Out

I have just spoken out to someone I love
Not knowing whether it's too far above
If this love is meant for me
Then it will appear for all to see

It was such a relief to let go of this emotion
Giving way to impulse I threw away caution
Expressing all that I felt for him
Hoping that love would fire within

I await with hope for that precious call
Without my friends around me I know I would fall
They support the inner strength inside
Helping to remember that love never dies

Love and Beauty are always around you
So have faith in everything that you do
Never taking anything for granted
Positivity will blossom as surely as the seed is planted

So I am still awaiting that call
No longer building any walls
When this chapter of my life ends
Life will open another door and my heart will mend

Awakening

Everything is getting too much for me
No one will open their eyes to see
I have let my head rule my life for too long
When all I want to do is seriously wrong

Breaking down in tears, it is me that I miss
Telling myself there is more to life than this
Deeper I delve to find my true self
Awakening the inner me that's been left on the shelf

We must not let the past rule the here and now
For everyone, freedom of choice we should allow
Never judging or criticising those souls
That don't fit our egotistical goals

Fellow peace and harmony is at hand
If you can place a foot on each piece of land
Let your higher self be your guide
For a loving heart and a spiritual mind

Dreams

Dreams are glorious and filled with light
Bubbles of joy in the darkness of night
Floating along in the realms of sparkle
Fluffy white clouds closing out garble

Bodies are weightless yet filled with love
Joining our higher self way up above
Two kinds of reality we should live
Unconditional loving we try to give

Opportunities will come and pass us by
Sometimes we regret and wonder why
So forgo the past and live for now
Lost opportunities we'll never think how

Let our life flow with creative joy
Express our inner light don't be coy
Our burdens will free themselves with ease
To enable a life full of harmony and peace

Inner contentment we will achieve
Throw away obstacles and be free
Never be afraid we are together
Brothers and sisters all one forever

I Love You

My love for you knows no bounds
All that I need, in you I have found
Walking into my life from out of the blue
I hope one day you feel the same way I do

You said you were following your own life path
With a soulful look and a sensuous laugh
Agreeing that our paths have now crossed each other
I fear the day if we have to leave one another

You know that I care, but not how much
My heart yearns for that moment when we touch
We sat there together and saw the shooting star
So close to each other and yet so far

The time will soon come for me to say
Those three little words come what may
I pray for the day you feel the way I do
When I look deep in your eyes and say, I Love You

Chance

Take a chance to see what you can gain
As all that I give is pleasure, not pain
So open yourself and let new luck roll
Let love and light into your soul

Your soul is a flame of eternal life
The fountain of youth easing the strife
Relax into the state of your sub conscious mind
Don't let the troubles of today be unkind

Live in the present and flow with ease
As calm underneath as the turbulent seas
Relieve all vibes of pressure and stress
It's time to think, positive more, negative less

A positive attitude is a positive outcome
So clear all negativity and become as one
Carry yourself with a tranquil serenity
Centre within and live a life of quality

Letting Go

I know that you love me, though you can't say
What is meant for us will soon come our way
You have been hurt many times in the past
Yet I know in my heart this love will always last

You know that I love you so very much indeed
The yearning to be with you is more than a need
You are caring to me in all that you do
And all I have I give to you

I am to you that wonderful woman you say
That came bouncing into your life on a bright sunny day
You are for me that perfect man
In our time together you'd protect me when you can

Wherever you go and whatever you do
You know that I would be still and wait for you
Past pains should be forgotten from both our lives
So that we can live our life with harmonious vibes

At Night

We spent many a fun day and night
Joining together our perfect light
Opening my heart you filled it with song
We were there as us, now we are gone

Back we move to our separate homes
But now I am feeling all alone
I toss and turn throughout the night
Sleep evades as you come into sight

With your sensitive eyes so beautiful and deep
You tell me at night you can't sleep
We realise with our minds that we have to go slow
Yet in our hearts we truly know

Why do we put ourselves through pain
When we know united all we do is gain
Free all our burdens and live in pleasure
As what we have can never be measured

Mind, Body and Soul

Your lips are so soft and sweet
Soulful eyes so brown and deep
Fingers caressing me gentle and firm
Making my body tingle and burn

Our bodies melt together as one
The enjoyment we feel is more than fun
Our breathing is getting heavy and fast
Inhibitions and thoughts are left in the past

Passion and love are set alight
Flaming as bright as the stars at night
Dizzy peaks we make each other touch
The energy we create is never too much

Holding one another emotions run strong
Hugging each other for the need is long
Lying close beside me your warmth is comforting
Giving what we need, unconditionally loving

You make me feel so warm and safe
Natural femininity with you I embrace
Mind, Body and Soul I hand over to you
Making me feel whole is what you do

No More

I can't believe this is happening to me
I thought our love was meant to be
You are falling out of love that I can see
This pain I'm feeling is killing me

You said you were scared of the way you feel
It's something with which you have to deal
So the loving ends and being friends takes place
Tears I cry as I see your face

Two people who love each other and yet apart
Is a waste of emotion from the heart
Friendship you want, that you can have
Anything else for us is too far above

All that I have I would give to you
To receive, you know what you have to do
Good friends is what you want us to be
I don't know if my heart will hold out for me

My love for you will not cease to grow
Just as the sea will continue to flow
You are for me that everything
Now and forever you will be my king

Watching you walk out that door
Knowing that you can give me no more
Hoping one day you walk back into my life
As this pain is cutting me like a knife

Goodbye

I met you once after all this time
Never forgetting those committed crimes
Emotion now gone I looked into your eyes
Wondering why at the tears I cried

When I look back I try to find what I saw
That made me love you, more than anyone before
As hard as I search, nothing I find
Now I am clear in my heart and my mind

I have come along way and so have you
Building our lives in the way that we do
You have found a new love and so have I
Soon it will be time to say our final goodbye

I wish you well in your new family life
Creating a foundation for your wedded wife
Maybe one day we will talk again
But this is now and that will be then

Leaving each other was the best thing we did
It was a relationship that was doomed to be
So now that the love has eventually died
It is time for me now to say Goodbye

Materialism

It's the same old routine every day
Not enough time to go out and play
We work so hard to buy those things
House, Car, Clothes and Rings

We are born into this world with nothing
Except a strong united family loving
In our childlike era everything is possible
Not knowing fear only aware of being capable

Guided by tradition to form our views
Our only worry is what we can lose
Our minds become prisons with society's pressures
Adults now, gone the days of younger pleasures

So what we have, the choice is ours
We can live on this earth and reach for the stars
Can material objects bring you happiness
Only you can decided this is not a test

Happiness can be defined in many ways
All I say is make the most of each day
Never dwell on yesterday or tomorrow
Hold onto your dreams and watch yourself go

You will leave this world onto another
The possessions you gained are of no matter
Honesty and Trust are your most valuable assets
So make you choice and place your bets

Adele (Citrus Cafe)

We've spent many a moment at the Citrus Café
Listening to each other on what we have to say
In the day we drink coffee and at night we drink beer
Always there for one another expressing our inner fear

We have sat there crying, tears of joy and pain
Wondering sometimes if we are going insane
But most of all we've shared that fun contagious laughter
Watching and meeting people, finding in life what they're after

Plenty of food and music we have now definitely consumed
In our Mediterranean place where sadness refuses to loom
Conversations are full of spiritual fulfillment
Emotional support at hand when each other's has been spent

So what would I do without my spiritual soul mate
But to continue my life and deal with fate
You've been there for me and I'm here for you
No matter where we go and no matter what we do

You have many many qualities so special indeed
You're not tainted by materialism, hatred or greed
Understanding and caring is the kind of person you are
I love you as a friend no matter how near or far

Karen

We've known each other now for quite awhile
Safe in our knowledge that we make each other smile
We've helped each other through the bad times that come
Making ourselves strong so we can be at peace as one

You love to hear all about my life packed days
Making you laugh with my impulsive ways
What you don't know is that I enjoy to say
Sharing those times with you in every way

You make me laugh with your hot headed manner
With your assertiveness and logic I don't see in any other
Just thinking of you brings a smile to my face
As you bring a ray of sunshine into every place

Thank you so much for being a wonderful friend
I know that our friendship will never end
Always remember to be positive in every way
Finding pleasure in life's opportunities come what may

Just be yourself and continue to be
Life will unfold when it's time for you to see
Face life head on and never run for cover
Closing one door will always open another

Freedom

Have you ever wondered what it is like to be free
To come and go and do as you please
Freedom of choice to do as you wish
To let life touch you as soft as a kiss

Are your feet itching to move from solid ground
To leave each place without so much as a sound
Travel the world to see what you can achieve
Going from place to place, wondering at sights you see

Is this a goal in life or are you running from within
Problems you will encounter, everyone is akin
Sometimes all that is required is a fresh start
So enjoy your life with a balance of head and heart

It is not as confusing as you might think so
Grab each opportunity as it comes and just go
Free as a bird soaring high in the sky
Learning to let each problem just pass you by

Soulmates

Can you imagine what it did to me
To find in you the me I see
It's like meeting your double, is this fate
Or are you truly and spiritually my life's soulmate

You think and feel the way that I do
A miracle it seems I found in you
To converse mentally and emotionally in the way that we feel
Our actions speak louder, words have no deal

So perceptive we are when we come together
A spiritual bonding we have for each other
We can read one another with just our eyes
Truth and Honesty unite, there's no need for lies

What we have is unique and ought to be cherished
Compassion a fragrance that can truly be lavished
Our auras burst open with receptive power
Kindred souls beautiful and free like a flower

What we have together can never be lost
Sacrifices are made whatever the cost
Enter through that unlocked gate
As you will always be my loving soulmate

Your Princess

You are and will be ultimately the best
Your life is full of energy and zest
But you still find time to be there for me
Why has it taken me so long to see

Creative talents flow through you with purity
Expressing yourself with emotional clarity
Depth and understanding you hold within you
Knowing exactly where you go and what you do

Those times when you were beside me are so long ago
You were my tower of strength when I needed you so
My love for you is a deep rooted feeling
I've learnt a lot from you, thank you for being

So a few years have passed and we do what we have to
We met together briefly, it was so good to see you
Your always in my thoughts, though our contact is less
And I know in your heart I'm forever your Princess

Integration

I feel as one within myself
I have reached the ultimate in spiritual wealth
Integration has happened of my two minds
The inner turmoil no longer winds

Completion is a centered jewel
Shining so bright, I have endless fuel
This overwhelming peace and inner contentment
Is given freely to others as it's never spent

Watching the fire as it grows around you
Spreading to others as you do
Their lives becoming peaceful and serene
We are living in reality, though it feels like a dream

My head is empty and my body is calm
As if someone has touched me with soothing balm
Having no worries and experiencing no fears
Completely in control, no shedding of tears

What I have gained it is simplistic to say
People only want when they have lost their way
Don't leave it to late before you climb that path
Start your journey now with a smile and joyful laugh

Creation

To hold our baby in my arms
To keep him warm and safe from harm
The swell of pride boiling up inside
Emotions run strong, I do not hide

Such a responsibility we now have
Dependent for his nourishment, food and love
This baby of ours has no fears or qualms
We sway him gently like the Caribbean palms

A bundle of joy created from our love
Our amazement speechless on what we have
This fragile child so delicate and sweet
His gripping fingers and tiny pink feet

All pain forgotten as I hold our son
Awaiting those days of sadness and fun
We will give him guidance but let him learn
That wisdom comes from every twist and turn

The most precious asset that we now can give
Is an appreciation to enjoy the way you live
To accept the things that life gives to you
And to see enjoyment and simplicity in all that you do

Father

My father you are, in ways I don't know
I look back in life I and have nothing to show
Except a fear of loss and maybe dependency
And a loving son for all the world to see

I try and learn from your trusted culture
Yet I know temptation did you lure
Not showing if you were there for me
The doors are no longer shut as I have the key

Doing and being as I am
Wanting for you to understand
But your eyes are blank and your head is gone
To your tropical land where the sun always shone

Your illness is there throughout your days
A special person you are in your own different way
I cannot explain the emotions I feel
They spin inside me like a magical wheel

To your blessed day I will care for you
And after, in my thoughts, in all that I do
A good father I will become as I see your growth
Brighter paths I now travel with trust and faith

I am nearly at one within myself
Caring about my finances, emotions and health
I have come a long way in the last year
To live a better life, lighter and happier, without fear

Are You or Aren't You

I look back at the men I have known in the past
Wondering why none of them could last
They didn't hold those qualities I desire
Unable to ignite my spark into a fire

Upon thinking maybe I never gave them a chance
Too greedy for life to give a second chance
But now I have stopped, as you I have found
Only for you to put my feet back on the ground

I wonder why you make it difficult for us
When I express my love, you just make a fuss
I have realized what a great woman I am
So strong and independent I achieve what I can

I have wonderful qualities inside of me
Sometimes I think you just cannot see
Are you taking me for granted, for what you can
Or are you really a truly loving man

Strangers remark, "I wish I had a woman like you"
That puts the beauty in life the way that you do
Please open your heart and your mind to see
And set yourself right and head towards me

I need you to appreciate me much more that you do
To express yourself verbally and say you love me too
Show me the respect and consideration I deserve
Don't make this relationship into a never ending curve

Breakthrough

I don't know what the hell I'm doing
All I seem to be is to-ing and fro-ing
I am in this so called relationship
My life should be happy but it is a tip

He wants to be deep, emotional and physical
But he will not knock down that brick wall
I know he loves me, or so he claims
Or is he leading me down those lanes

Six months on and I wonder where we are
Whether we are growing together or afar
Now he is stressed out and needs his space
So where does that leave me in this god-forsaken place

Right now I also have something on my mind
And I don't know whether to be cruel or kind
There's a possibility of a pregnancy here
And I could lose all that I hold dear

So no matter what I am going through
For him and his problems I will always be true
Putting his life before my very own
But I always end up being alone

So right not I am holding my peace
My patience ongoing, never to cease
I have decided that giving freely I can no longer do
I have to be true to myself as well as you

Running Away

I feel like running away
There is no reason for me to stay
What's the point in all this pain
I have absolutely nothing to gain

The Caribbean is the place calling me
There is always one person I want to see
He gives me everything I need
Some people might call this a dirty deed

To give up on this man I claim to love
But what I want with him I cannot have
I am feeling tired and think I'm wasting time
As I sit here and wait for his special sign

Don't get me wrong I love him indeed
Regardless of race, colour or creed
I want to be held each and every night
I don't need a bird of fancy who will just take flight

I am still in a dither, so when in doubt do nowt
When I make a decision I must do it with clout
So god help him when the time comes for me
As there is no going back when it's the world I want to see

Eclipse

Watching the eclipse of the moon tonight
A few lonely stars manage to shine their light
The power of the planets creating their force
Mystic wonders for mother natures' cause

The shadowy effect magnetically pulling
Illusionary clashing of the planets still moving
Clouds now drift thick and heavy
Yet the planet earth remains just as a steady

Emotional depths rise up inside
The rush overwhelming as a creative tide
Losing my head in the spark of magic
Watching the moon flicker like a candle wick

The moon has now gone to the other side
This is the only place it now may hide
Just as you wonder will you see the face again
Glimpses of light appear to shine on women and men

Soon you will think it has all been a dream
Because nothing appears to be what it seems
Moonlight shadows are all around
The moon high in the sky and me on the ground

Suspension

I feel like I am being suspended
My whole life has been upended
Sometimes I'm so physically drained
No wonder, look at all I have gained

I pour all my energy into everything I do
Maybe I am being a stupid fool
Giving all that I have to this
Never receiving anything, making a dark abyss

Only I can pull myself out of this hole
I have to stop digging like a mole
All I want is peace and harmony
To have a loving partner and just be

I have to make a move I can't stay still
Draw on that inner strength and find my will
I need to have purpose in my life again
I have to make decisions, where and when

Remembering that when I close that door
I can then start receiving more
There's no point in staying in this space
I need to move onto a brighter place

Holy Matrimony

We have both experienced many times of pain
The sun never shining only seeing the rain
Leaving the past right where it belongs
Our hearts and souls are now filled with song

You came into my life like a breath of fresh air
Leaving me dizzy and without a care
Very quickly I realized what you mean to me
To have you love me for the way I am meant to be

This love has grown strong and is filled with happiness
The passion is burning when our lips meet and kiss
We are here for each other to support, care and honour
You are my life, I don't need any other

We are now being joined in holy matrimony
And I know in our hearts we will never be lonely
Soon we will move into our marital home
This will be our foundation of bricks and stone

I am the luckiest woman in all of the world
I want to shout as loud as I can, I want to be heard
I love you so very much my darling husband
Forever and Eternity we will walk hand in hand

Caribbean Skies

I sit here in the sun and watch the waves flow by
They crash on rocks or they just die
The ocean quiet with a force of energy
Awaiting Mother Nature to unleash her demonic fury

The clouds are tinged with grey and anger
Swirling the sea against the rocks, now harder
The sun has gone to shine elsewhere
Leaving us now in the mouth of its lair

In the distance there is nothing but empty darkness
We hope and pray that maybe it will pass us
The wind is gathering its almighty pull
To feed below ensuring its survival

The time is here, she has complete control
The lightening flashes and the thunder rolls
The sea and sky unite as one
The day as we know it has now gone

The sky is streaked with electric colours
As the lightening bolts and the sea is smothered
Piercing through the thunderous cloud
Smooth as silk and yet not a sound

The storm is heightening, yet beauty is still
Energy pulsating to do as it will
Absorbing the power I look into its eyes
Nothing beholden to the Caribbean skies

Michelle

You are the dearest friend to me
The special qualities that only you can see
Allowing me to gather strength for myself
To help me live with joy and health

With your own heart and mind in turmoil
You remain to me so very loyal
Putting aside your innermost fears
You are there for me guiding, supportive and to hear

The beauty that is held deep within you
Shines like a light in all the things that you do
Your emotional tides of depth and feeling
Leave the marks of your magical healing

What you have is unique and ought to be cherished
Compassion is a fragrance that can truly be lavished
Blossom my friend like the flower you are
Open to love, light and life to go far

When the Rain Falls

When the rain falls I cry my tears
This is my way of losing all my fears
You caused me so much hurt and pain
I won't let you put me through this again

The bad times now outweigh the good
It's time for me to cut away the dead wood
That's why you see me packing my case
It's time for me now to leave this place

I shall start my life afresh and new
A million miles away from you
I realize now I have so much to give
For me and for others I intend to live

Never will I wish you ill-harm
Everyone holds their own charm
I forgive you for all you have said and done
The love I held for you has now gone

When the rain falls I will no longer cry
Love will come again I won't hesitate to try
I will think and learn from the past
Then I will find happiness at last

New Journey

I have no idea where to begin
You impacted my life with a zing
With your soulful eyes and sensuous lips
My knees go weak and my heart flips

What we have together feels completely right
No guilt attached only love and light
We talk and listen to each other
Kindred souls beautiful and free like flowers

This path we travel is young and new
Our feelings like birds, we took off and flew
This journey is a mystery tour
That has been discovered and should be explored

My feelings grow for you day to day
On a path that I thought I had lost the way
So fearful am I at being hurt once more
I'm scared to open that loving door

Yet I believe you can help me be
The person I yearn for, me
Lift those barriers that cover me round
Let's join together and be found

Kitchen Aromas

We've spent many a moment on your kitchen floor
Listening to each other on what we have to say and more
In the day we drink tea and at night we drink wine
Always there for one another, everything seems fine

We have sat there crying, our tears of joy and pain
Wondering sometimes if we are going insane
But most of all we've shared, that fun contagious laughter
Watching and meeting people, finding in life what their after

Plenty of wine and music we have now consumed
In your warm kitchen where sadness refuses to loom
Conversations are full of spiritual enlightenment
Emotional support at hand when each other's has been spent

So what would I do without my spiritual soul mate
But to continue our lives and deal with fate
You've been there for me and I'm here for you
No matter where we go and no matter what we do

Time to Leave

Gone are the days and nights we shared
You and I, for each other we cared
Memories are all that we now hold
Our paths going separate ways, we must be bold

It's now time for our final goodbye
No longer next to you will I lie
My love for you will always be strong
The timing for you was just so wrong

For us to work, needed both you and me
I was ready, but you just wanted to be
In my heart and soul is a special place for you
And always will be, you just need to see it too

My thoughts and emotions will always be with you
I hope that someday you will think of me too
A healthy balance of head and heart can be your guide
Don't sit at the ocean bottom, flow with the tide

So my dearest one it's time to say farewell
You warmed my soul and my passion you did quell
It's time to move on through that open gate
Maybe my darling, for you, it's not too late

Nature's Way

The flowers sway gentle in the breeze
My skirts billowing softly against my knees
Wandering barefoot through the grass
Feeling as one with nature at last

Gathering my skirts with a smile I go
Running in the sun carefree without a woe
My hair streaming behind me wild and free
A spring in my step and my heart full of glee

My surroundings are peaceful, lush and green
Illuminous in the powerful ray of the sun's beam
The wondrous glory of all that is around us
Hearing the birds sing and the sound of the bees buzz

Tears come to my eyes as the gentle wings
Of approaching butterflies harmoniously sing
The warmth of nature at her best
This life so simple yet full of zest

Standing there now, so quiet and still
Looking much further towards the hills
Feeling the power of nature's surroundings
Stretch out your arms to give yourself wings

Hold your head high and open your eyes
To see the tranquility in the sky
The breeze and sun caressing your face
No one else here in your own private place

Imagine as you will where you can go
Release your anxieties nice and slow
Taking deep breaths fill your lungs with air
And lift yourself up and fly, without a care